Evening Oracle

LETTER MACHINE EDITIONS   TUCSON, AZ

Evening Oracle

Brandon Shimoda

Published by Letter Machine Editions

Tucson, Arizona 85721

© 2015 by Brandon Shimoda

Cover Art: from a postcard of a young Japanese entertainer (date
    unknown), from a collection titled "Sekaiichi Kuma-musume" (The
    World's Greatest Bear Girl), archived at the Tohoku Culture Research
    Center, Tohoku University of Art & Design (Yamagata, Yamagata).

All Rights Reserved

Book Design by HR Hegnauer

Printed in the USA

Cataloging-in-Publication Data is on file at the Library of Congress

ISBN: 978-0-9887137-5-8

lettermachine.org

Distributed to the trade by Small Press Distribution (spdbooks.org)

On the first page of my songs is a strange engraving. It still has a faint smell of ink. I see a shadow in the copper oxide, verdigris: a lovely shadowy being walks through the visionary trees … I am walking.

TWO WOMEN. RESPECTS NEVER STOP. TAMAMUSHI. ETSUKO. SATSUKI. TAMAMUSHI. CAMPHOR TREE. CAMPHOR TREE, OTOYO. TONOSHO. SHIJO-OHASHI. INASAYAMA. TSURUNOYU. NAGASAKI. MASAKO. O BON. TSURUNOYU. TOYOTOMI HIDEYORI, YODO-DONO, MOTHER AND SON.   AFRICA MARU. NAKANOSE, BLACK FLAGS, FIVE HERON. EELS AND CATFISH by HIROMI ITO.

But what I really wanted to tell you. My grandmother died this morning. Whenever I think about my "personal" history. It is 9:18 in the morning in the San Fernando Valley. Those oranges remind me. Today, on the phone I thought I heard, for the first time. Your father's voice, because he touched the living wire. Returned last night from an unexpected 6 day trip. But, you all were there talking. the trip back on Sunday. We spoke on the phone the week she died. If there was ever a settlement for pure autonomous belief. I do think I can name the women. I'm furious with myself for taking so long. And I was so pleased to meet your father and grandmother. We said goodbye to Grams for the day. I just a few nights ago attended to my granddad as he died. We bought Grandad his exercise bike. I was in a room in a house. Hiromi told me that she really hoped that you would not be offended. Oh, that is such

a good idea, two trees that have grown next to each other.
No, I never think of the pink lady. All things now to begin in
O. The past two weeks have been defined by erosion. Sending
you more poems than is appropriate. Here's the "watermelon"
poem I mentioned. I want "The Japanese Apricot." It feels
like coming. We're driving out to California not this coming
weekend, but the next. We spread part of my mom's ashes in
a lake. My grandmother lived in the San Fernando Valley.
Today is my grandmother's funeral. Dear Brandon, her ashes
really look like a cloud. As I was walking up the stairs. I
neglected to tell you that the very last thing.

THE JAPANESE APRICOT. TOHOKU.
SUGAWARA NO, MICHIZANE. KEYAKI, KEYAKI,
KEYAKI. KEYAKI. HITOTSUBASHI GAKUEN.
TODAIJI. NINNAJI. IKEDA. AKAMA. KANSAI
REHABILITATION. TANI HOUSE. ♿. EGGPLANT.
KAMO. TETSUGAKU. THREE POEMS by DOT
DEVOTA. SHIRAKAMI. TWO MEN. MOTOYASU.
MOMIJIDANI. MIYAJIMA. MOTOYASU. EVENING
ORACLE. YOKOHAMA.

TWO WOMEN

Two women on the slope of a mountain
One coming down the other going up
The mountain eclipsing the sky so briefly
Even the most vigilant miss it

The woman coming down is balancing a dead baby on her head
The woman going up has a dead baby strapped to her back
The woman coming down is wearing a white robe with salmon
    undergarments
The woman going up is wearing a salmon robe with gray
    undergarments

RESPECTS NEVER STOP

A woman burned into the slope of a mountain
Deposits black eggs up the skirts of women passing
To admire pink flowers growing cool through wild coal
Feel nothing but what thereafter is shared
Of the burn, if anything, impatient for proof
Pink flowers so small they hardly matter

And yet, never stop
Yet respects
Never stop   Eggs glistening
As they roll down the mountain

TAMAMUSHI

The wing of a small pond
In a daughter's hand
Days are meant to unfold

Or fold
Or fly or
Drowning, die

You see, there is something
Rare in the air or
Open, fits

One life
To it
And that is yours

And you know it
And still don't care
The fight is over, that has been made

Clear, though
Not without
Enough. You went off

ETSUKO

Etsuko paints faces on rocks
She finds
A simpler credulity

One rock wears a hat
With a pink stripe and a yellow stripe
Etsuko encountered in a major mountain system

One rock is a man, as such
Is a baby. It is his baby that knows
The world before him

One rock resembles a pig
A pig, Etsuko says, with a coquettish face
And peasant's bonnet

A sensitive and triangular face
In the mirror, a person deserving attention
Crystal in magic

One rock resembles a warrior
Walking through a field toward the sea

The sea is inhuman, how about you
Let me paint eyes on your nipple ...
How many live there? How many used to?

Etsuko has rocks woven into her walls
Heavy, her house carries
Away night

Fires, stars
The back of a neck
Painted with a free hand

Etsuko's rocks look good when catching
Rain, and when the rain
Pulls off

SATSUKI

Satsuki is ninety. Seventy years ago, she married a man
With a very large nose
That day the sun rose white, or did it
Set?   People swimming in the sun were beautiful
And even though a modest detail of the ensemble
Satsuki's husband's nose
Was very large

It is now
A pile of lice

. . .

Satsuki feeds us watermelon
Pours us energy drink
Then lies down on the floor
And stares at the ceiling

Her husband's face
Above the vase of plastic flowers

Death's possessive

. . .

Satsuki remembers whispering into her husband's nose
Let's pull candy
From a cloud! Then grow like lice
Not out of loneliness   The cloud showered
Honest feeling
Directly through the ceiling

. . .

When Americans ran their boat aground
Satsuki walked across the sand
And asked them, Are you summer school?
The Americans descended like frogmen from the boat
Stood inspecting the crabs
And breast-like vegetables

. . .

Where the watermelon is bathed
In sweat on a dish
In a room in a house on a hill, people are garrulous
Ask many questions
Go multiple times to the toilet

. . .

When Satsuki bends
To say Goodbye
The room bends around her
Ninety year-old cleavage

The sun withdraws

Satsuki holds her arms
Above her head
In the gesture of a solar charioteer

With the sound a woman makes
Impersonating the sun

Beating life
In an arc to the underworld

TAMAMUSHI

Waking is dying often
Feels exactly how
It feels

To fly to the center of where it is
To stake a claim on silence or
Murmur, This is the realm

I have been made
I have been told
To make

CAMPHOR TREE

On the shore of a small pond
Beneath a camphor tree
A monk set himself on fire

A solution ran clean
Through his mind
Projecting a rectangle in space

Where he placed his meditation

Why do we look admiringly upon the smoke
Rising
A dark, unwinding veil?

Would it be
Intimate

To set ourselves on fire
Become the anonymous
Veil over the water

CAMPHOR TREE

When the eight hundred year-old tree
Is viewed in a single moment
Eight hundred spirited communications
Divide the tree
Into eight hundred inspiriting moments
Leaving less than one
To decide what is
Carrying each moment of life

When the poet comes to each of the eight hundred years
The poet becomes the tree's offspring

The tree commits a cell of itself
To the poet's psyche

. . .

Where a monk took his life
Beneath the tree
And became a shabby corsage
In a cup, I am pissing   The colors rise up
Form a transient poem in the air

OTOYO

The poet pisses
On the feet of the family, folded in
Reverential style

TONOSHO

On the bend of a narrow road
Over a guardrail
Trees
Below flowers
The canopy

The only tree alive
With butterflies
At the top
Vouchsafed
And they're all blue

Butterflies
A darker shade
The sea forms gracious
Psyche wind

Tall American says
Howdy to Americans
Though tall cannot
Reach to screw so
Jerks alone without light

Other butterflies reach
Their end
Other less
Picturesque
Castrations

Perhaps the light is obscure
Not seeming to be
Instrumental

To aerate a metaphor
Is important
To be straight with what
You are not looking
At also

I found butterflies in
A cave, butter

In butterfly-shaped holes

There! A butterfly on a thistle
Dancing better
Than all the other
Angers in this
Medium

The narrow road
Crumbles
White stars
In the weeds
Hot as mirrors

SHIJO-OHASHI

Without forgetting
I am a child

Standing on a bridge in the old
Imperial capital

Looking up at the heads and
Beyond heads the hills

Are on fire   The sun is touching
The earth

The first strike burns

Those standing shadowless
Between a thick singling

All the way through to the sun, turning in
Apprehension, for the sun need not replicate

My feet are no longer
Touching the bridge that
Was earlier

Come on night
Have I really been
Inside you?

. . .

The bodies of thousands
Contain me against them

I read fires on the swell
For the first time out loud

I hold my hand above the crowd

Appear as offspring from

Divine collision   Having won!
And having each

Concentration of the sun
Nerves the fires

. . .

To come back I have been talking
About learning to see
With learning to speak
I am learning

To perfume the air
With carbonation and meat

Will I be alert as ion supply?
Moving with a can of fruit tucked inside?
Just taking the sun from one crown to another?

. . .

When I am sick I am well
When I have eaten too many fruits
Before noon I am hungry

I am full when I want to listen to music
Guitars simultaneously heavy
Playing air as a liquid

When I arrive I am nervous
About this old man's ass, this young girl on the train
I fall in love with this old man's ass, this young girl on the train

INASAYAMA

Go to the island, climb the sweet potato
You will see the carcinogenic lights, yes
But do not simply look at what bewitches you
Pay attention also to the heron rose
Spreading the shape of a horse, the rabbit
Struck by a bolt of live woodening, the horse
Growing out of the luna whipping sugar
Out of hands, idle hands

Pay attention also to the shadows, how they attest
To the frankness of murder

TSURUNOYU

One dreams of living above a bathhouse
In a snow-covered field
With a procession of white animals
Passing nightly
An uncanny flame

A white bear, a white pelican, a white rabbit
Another white bear
The remnants of an army

Who is one?
One spends evenings
At a small desk in a small room
In a small building above
A bathhouse

What is it to dreams?
Dreams hang ladders down

mint-scented waters

What is a bathhouse?
The moon shines on
The back of my neck
Disappears into my throat

White animals rise
In echoes of a simple, arcane heat
Rewriting each night
Each night

NAGASAKI

The asses of old men
Coming out of the bath, I admire
And am suddenly reminded, I miss
And I missed, the garden of asses
Shooting off in the open

Lowering into the garden, I am suddenly reminded ...

A break in the weather
Is justification
Or all that is needed   Clouds simply parting

. . .

An old woman with a towel over her eyes
Selling rosewater ice cream
To those who've arrived
To stand in the shadow of the bomb
Is sleeping
Beneath a large tree   a small cart with a metal chest resting
In the path, tall towers of sugar cones

The limbs of the tree outline membranous shapes
The old woman feels
Washed out   Why can't she live
To touch the minds

The bomb touched
The final feet? Surely the bomb was alone?

MASAKO

Fog encircling a mountain
Every eye small, but what is seen
For real? The song
Played at one's funeral?
A lovelorn feeling? No, the fog
Adult and expanding

. . .

One joins a cult
And loses touch
With those who disapprove
But they are lively, or so
Is said   They barely move

. . .

Masako runs the public bath
Sees everyone without clothes
Hands out soap, razors, the paper, white towels
Small things to bite down on

I give Masako a copy of *O Bon*, the book I wrote

Dreaming of my grandfather, or the version of my grandfather

I was dreaming of

That brought me

Out of the dream, the book

She touches, says, has *O Bon* thrown pain?

Has *O Bon* tricked anyone into thinking

Pain is not that, but that pain over there

While here I can suddenly move?

The fog has lifted   I can love and be loved?

O BON

Across the surface of the river, soldiers
Stepping lightly
The first steps are easy

The water cleanly divides
Callus lily and flesh
Stems tied to the bow of a boat

Pushing off
    river water

A mirror strung along
The shore in which the boat becomes
Two boats   The glance of

The oarsman exactly as
The glance of the oars
      in the glass

Each man's eyes
At the place where they should be
On the other man's face

Each man's hands

Expanding in the curve

Each man gathers the load of the river
Into his arms

The muscles in each oarsmen's arms
Fray each of the oarsmen's arms
From shoulder to finger

Roughly equal

Water cannot be grasped
Or filled by any arm

As for the wood of each
Oar it is
Chestnut

Each man's hands
As each man's arms
If the sky is not asked in advance

TSURUNOYU

I sit in the mint. My heart has a bubble
An old man tells me not to go in
Above my heart, I have gone in above my heart
I am white, the fog is judicious, the mountain a splendor
But who will remember
What I looked like?

The old man
Cocks his head

I stare at his recumbent testicle

TOYOTOMI HIDEYORI

I jump with my mother
Into the mythology of the nation
When on all sides storms
Swallow power

I notice the hair on my mother's ear, wonder
Does it also hear wind? Or with
A slight vestige of madness there
Now no more distance?

YODO-DONO

I jump with my son into the mound
No one will remember, no one will recover
The mound will never disclose

And yet, the wind
With no violation of right
Might carry us beyond
Our shadows seized upon

MOTHER AND SON

Find the source of restlessness
In a restful aesthetic   Not restfulness, fortitude
Immersed in ground color
While an edge
Writes a greater edge

A son captured and beheaded
A daughter sent to the garden
To become a father

We went to Japan
To find the source of our restlessness
In an aesthetic of rest

Enshrined in malnourished love and hate

Bred into incriminating fictions of loving
And hating

Between the circle and the mound there is a person
Between the person and the mound is early morning
Between early morning and the mound
There is a foreshock

Heat invertebrate maturation of a species

                              Ceramic of the ashes
Circle taking out the river and the trees
Sight, inside out
A day like any other

Will the person become a circle?
Will the person become a mound, part of the mound?
Will the person recover   will the person be recovered?

Hell   Family is from hell
Where only you are
Made of hell
Mother, father, sisters, never

STATES they are, STATES you don't
Hate is hell where you are right
Behind you, pressing against you STATES

Thinking happens sudden
Absorbing women and children enshrined in earth

Dig until people find it
Enter and be torn
Sit on the neck   is time, quiet
Loins, highborn existence

A man with white helmet in blue
Walks across the mound, scalps the grass
Keeps it sensible, picturesque

A man on the wall in a dress
A man on the wall   dress on skin

No dress, no man   first palpitation

To envision with clothes   to see with clothes
To see hot contours on a wall
Restored and want to mount it

If arrested in the process of becoming an American
You will be forever-most American
Exile-assumption masked as faith, repeating
The first attempt to mate

AFRICA MARU

A plum falls into the sea
From a branch overhanging a migrant
Surrounded by the sea   Brides   The plum
Falls into
The brides
Take the migrant in
Their sleeves

The migrant exists only in a picture
As himself and himself in the one
He's going to meet

For the first time

The migrant is free

To choose   Is he actually free to choose?
His face in the face
Of another known only
In a picture

A plum falls from a branch
Into a sleeve   The migrant, surrounded by brides
Leaps into the sea, hangs on a low-hanging cloud
The brides hold pictures to their chests
Unfamiliar faces of men
They are going to meet

For the first time

Free to choose? Are they actually free to choose?

NAKANOSE

A heron rose
Then another heron rose
Then another heron rose
Then a fourth heron
Then a fifth

I could smell
Where each rose
Like a codex peeling
To the organ   Shimodas are buried here! Hiromi said
Here is one
Buried! Shimoda! And another!
Fallen in a field, surrounded by laughter, last vegetation

I can feel my vagrant idiocy
Mistranslating those
Unrelated to me
I visit still, repeatedly

BLACK FLAGS

A heron wrapped in a torn standard
While smaller herons like asterisks
Bathe in the flash——

FIVE HERON

Five heron rose, threading the sky

A good world
I wanted

But the heron
Were setting——

EELS AND CATFISH by HIROMI ITO

A strange e-mail arrived
Hello to you
My name is Shimoda
And I'm a poet
Writing from Western Maine
I am wondering
If you might have any
Recommendations or suggestions
Of places to visit in and around Kumamoto
I responded. What do you want of me?
That was the first time I had received an e-mail, had
        someone approach me
Someone I didn't know, just because I live in Kumamoto
I imagined this Shimoda fellow was hoping I'd be nice
And say, well then, why don't you stay with me?
But that is too presumptuous
Kumamoto summers are unbearably hot
Japanese houses are even hotter and more humid than the
        horrible weather outside
I hated the thought of taking in a complete stranger
But there was a day that I too had arrived like that
In an unfamiliar land
I ate the food that the people there had given me

I squandered the time the people there provided

I felt like I had to repay my debt

So although terribly busy, I went into town in the horrific heat

And picked him up

But he was not one person but two

A young man and a young woman

I took them both out to eat some soba

As I read the menu out loud, I convinced them

This is the most *oosentikku*

Japaniizu fuudo in this town

Although that is not entirely true

We don't know, we'll just leave it up to you, they said

Not bothering to ask their likes and dislikes, I settled on sea
    eel tempura with soba

(The restaurant was in the Tokyo style and was really good

But we were in Kumamoto, and unfortunately it didn't have
    mustard-stuffed lotus roots

Or boiled green onions with sour miso, or raw horsemeat

The kinds of local delicacies you would expect in Kumamoto)

The two began to talk as we waited

We are looking for a place, a place called Nakanose

That was the place my grandfather lived

We looked it up, and then, we found it

That place name has disappeared

We think we'll go there, take a bus

Today after we get done, they said

Their attitude, their wish to solve the problem themselves

Gave me a good impression

Plus, they were both really young

And come to think of it, he was not just a poet

He was a Japanese-American

Hold on a minute, I said

I called Baba-san

Baba-san is a friend of mine

A long time ago when I lost everything

When I was left behind, defenseless in Kumamoto

He came up to me smiling

And we have been doing things together ever since

As a civil servant, he has been transferred all over the prefecture

So he should know just about all the place names in Kumamoto

And as luck would have it, I got through to him in the middle
    of the day

I think you go along the Hamasen Bypass

And cross the Kase River, but hold on

I'll look it up, he told me

As they were eating their sea eel tempura and soba

And I was eating my junsai soba

Baba-san called back

I was right, go along the Hamasen Bypass, cross the Kase
    River, and it's there

He was right, the place name no longer exists

The name has been all but forgotten, it remains only in the
     name of a single restaurant
     "Tokunaga Eels, Nakanose Main Branch"

Put the telephone number in your GPS and you'll be sure to
     get there

Then Baba-san specified

That place is in Catfish

And so that is the way we went

As we left town, even after leaving town

There were rows upon rows of dull city streets

Then suddenly our path went down a narrow lane with
     nothing on it

Then the narrow lane gave way to a broad street

That was the Hamasen Bypass

Lined with boring city buildings

Rows of convenience stores and family restaurants

Rows of chain stores just like you might find anywhere

Rows of gaudy signs

Pachinko parlors raising a racket

Suddenly a large mall appeared

The parking lot stretching on endlessly

We crossed the bridge across the Kase River

At the foot of the bridge was a restaurant that specialized in eel

The aroma of barbequed eel filled the air

Beyond the restaurant was nothing but rice paddies

I stopped the car at the embankment and he walked around

Smoke was coming out of the eel restaurant

The air was full of a delicious scent

But he nor his wife didn't know

That scent came from the barbequed eels

That the scent alone makes you want to eat and eat

When his grandfather was nine

He set out alone for America

His family had already gone, the reason

He was left behind alone was because he was sick

After he recovered, the nine year-old boy

Went alone from Kumamoto to Oita, then set sail for Yokohama

Changed boats in Yokohama, then arrived in San Francisco

All alone

In the rice paddies across the way was a cemetery

Can we go in there?

He asked hesitantly

Sure, let's do it

I told him we could take the car and go over there

The narrow farming road went on and on

The water flowed alongside unbroken

There was a board forming a bridge from the road to the cemetery

There were more than ten gravestones

And there I found it, a gravestone marked Shimoda, the same
    name as his

It must be a relative, a direct one or not, I could not be sure

But looking at the wide-open landscape around the rice paddies

I could imagine how stubborn society must be

I could imagine his had not been the main branch but an
    offshoot of the family

A branch family goes out into the world, it splits off

And the descendant of that family

In this case becomes a nine year-old boy

Crosses the Pacific, goes from Yokohama to Oita, then arrives
    in Kumamoto

All alone

And stands face to face

With the grave where generations of the Shimoda family are
    buried

Next to that

Is the grave of Takayuki Shimoda

An army sergeant who died in the 1940s

Killed on the battlefield in his early twenties

(I took a photo of it on my cell phone, just now as I searched
    for it

A picture of my dead aunt's face suddenly came up on the screen

My aunt who died just recently, I did not go to the funeral

My cousin sent it, I wanted to erase it, but I could not bring
    myself to do it

I have keep my aunt, her dead face, her corpse in my cell phone)

On the far side of the road was Catfish

The name of the place was written clear as day on the
   telephone pole
      "Catfish, Kashima Town, Mashiki County"

In ancient times, a caldera formed in Aso and collected lots
   of water

A big, big lake formed there, and a big, big catfish lived inside

The god Takeiwatatsu-no-mikoto came and ruled over the area

He kicked in the side of the lake with his feet

The water overflowed and ran out, running, running,
   running all over the place

It ran and ran

It swallowed everything up

Everything perished

The native catfish was alive though

Takeiwatatsu-no-mikoto killed it by cutting it up

He chopped it up

Into little pieces

The place was covered in blood, but the water washed it away

A piece of the catfish was washed to this distant place

So this place is called Catfish

They call it that even now

A tiny, mud-colored frog jumped

From the top of the plank bridge down below

Tiny, mud-colored frogs jumped in the muddy water

The water had retreated but the trees and grasses
And vines had grown, covering traces of blood
Covering the slaughter
A blue heron walked slowly in the green rice paddy
When I started the car
The Japanese-American turned
Looked over his shoulder
And waved at his own roots

Suffer
wild animals
of in the company
of their spinach

Little spinach,
communication
is the key

But what I really wanted to tell you was how deeply I was struck by the vision of those women dancing (at the Bon festival) in pink-and-white kimonos—for I once painted them! When I was five and six we lived in Hawaii and thus my first two teachers, kindergarten and first grade, were Japanese, and in the spring (I loved those teachers, perhaps they were part of the root system of my life-long obsession with Japan, a country I have never been to and never will, yet feel strongly as if I have lived a long life there)—in the spring there was a cherry blossom festival and we learned a cherry blossom festival dance and performed it on a float I think in some kind of parade, maybe not, maybe we just danced in the street, but my teacher suggested I paint a dance (I was a rather marvelous painter when I was five) and I painted a Japanese lady in a pink-and-white kimono! It was my masterpiece, they hung it downtown in a museum in a show of children's paintings, with another one I made of my grandmother, and Brandon, the painting of my grandmother is hanging in my apartment as I write this, but the painting of the dancers in pink-and-white kimonos I never saw again! It is lost forever, it exists only in my mind, a sneaky part of me thinks that perhaps my mother saved the one of my grandmother but thought the Japanese dancers in kimonos wasn't worth saving … though I SWEAR to you it was a better picture, as I said it was my masterpiece, I let the pink paint run to evoke the wavering of the dance, and the reason I am telling you this is because you just saw my painting in motion so I know you will believe me, because you have seen it.

My grandmother died this morning. My mom called at 12:44. She was eating ice cream. My grandmother's eyes were half-closed, her breaths spaced out … At one point, she opened her eyes and looked out the window. My mom asked what she was looking at, but my grandmother, who was having trouble breathing, could not answer. They removed the tube from her stomach. She was born in 1928. I hung a picture of her on the wall above our bed with a piece of masking tape. Then fell asleep. This morning I thought of writing a poem, and it feels important to tell you I thought of it, because it is, or can be, a very strange impulse. The title came first: *The Neptune Society.* My grandmother wanted, wants, to be cremated, and for her ashes to be released over the ocean. You wrote, *It is kind of comforting to hear them as a sea* …

Whenever I think about my "personal" history I realize I just need to keep changing the white cotton compresses on the wounds as they are saturated. Today … I felt the sort of aluminum leaves of the past like something difficult I had made that cut my fingers which distracted me from the gut wound. Facts are fake plants, the shape without the life, hard and made.

It is 9:18 in the morning in the San Fernando Valley, Southern California. The shadows are long on the grass, the grass coarse like hay. There is a stone geisha strumming the biwa, looking anguished. She is facing a small rock garden in the center of which sits a five-story pagoda. On the other side of the yard is a larger rock garden, with a single-story pagoda at the tail-end of a stream of small black pebbles. There are two palm trees, the sun shining directly through …

DD and I have been spending part of our days in the university library down the street … where my mom took classes when she was pregnant with me, 1978; she took a class on color theory …

At the moment there are six lemons on the table … we keep moving them around …

I have started to write about my grandparents' sex lives, on both sides …

How did it come to this? What kind of spell has the ocean cast, and what are the people becoming? And yet, there are orange and grapefruit trees EVERYWHERE, walking the alleyways around the valley like understanding the origins of choice, our hands becoming momentarily foreign as the juice dries on them, then thinking: we'll go that way!

There are orange trees everywhere.

My grandmother is in a nursing home down the street. My grandfather, who rarely speaks, is sitting in his chair in the corner. We weren't planning to stay so long, but we have nowhere to go. So, we're here filling the fridge with fresh oranges.

Those oranges remind me of what we found in our fridge when we woke up the next day after landing in Hong Kong for the very first time in 1972. Oranges were such a rare and expensive item when I was a child in Korea, so I was thrilled, but then once I sat down to eat them, I started to feel incredibly sad about being elsewhere. It was the first time I really understood what distance was, that I had moved to the distance, the place my father always departed to from Korea.

Today, on the phone I thought I heard, for the first time, a tiny quiver in my father's voice. It didn't come when he was describing how the hospital said they thought they'd done everything they could for my dying grandfather

but a minute or so later, when he said that my sister's daughters were out visiting he and my mother

that quiver in his voice—where did it come from

too easy to say it was the result of his sudden awareness, for the first time, of his own mortality

the structures birds make

men make houses and paint them from miles away

But who the fuck am i to say …

Do you think we'll all turn round when we die, like grapefruit, to be dipped into the sea's radiant glow …

Your father's voice, because he touched the living wire that made of him his own father, seeing you in his daughter's kids, right, if the living wire is connected as true. It takes at least one remove to clarify ...

Returned last night from an unexpected 6 day trip to Portland, where, among other things, I gathered 5 gallons worth of walnuts from under a tree near a trailer house parked on my family's land

I carried Wil on my back, as I bent over the ground, and picked up the walnuts and placed them in a white bucket

walnuts to be dried in the green shed in whose shade I would often eat a sandwich with my grandfather after we moved hundreds of yards of irrigation pipe, mid-summer, 1993

two days before gathering walnuts with Wil, I stood over my sleeping grandfather as he struggled to breathe—and he died twenty minutes later—minutes after Kisha read him 2 Ripley Hugo poems

minutes after my dad applied a layer of vaseline to his lips after the nurse turned him over and combed his hair

me, Kisha, my grandmother, and dad sat in the living room of their apartment the minute he passed away, alone, in his bedroom, and at the time I thought he would have preferred to slip out as we all sat there talking about how ruthless my grandmother's cats can be

even now, I think he would have preferred it—though

I swallow hard at the fact no one was beside him

how were we to know that was the time

But, you all were there talking ...

And maybe it needed to be a day, not necessarily an occasion. What do you remember now of your grandfather's skin and hair?

Picking up walnuts and bringing them to the green shed is also the circulatory of a day, not necessarily an occasion. Occasions are damaging, days, however evanescent, are the salve if we would have them.

the trip back on Sunday: airplanes and bodies and when I shut my eyes the differences in my grandfather's face before he died and after he died

his skin and hair

when I entered the room, an hour or so before he passed, and saw him there, asleep, breathing hard, I had the sense he was already gone

forty-five minutes into our flight I looked out the window (north) and saw the bitterroot valley, clear as day, from 37,000 feet

i could see the winding river I spent hours floating i could even see the southern edge of missoula

no deer on the hills

when we finally returned, i saw a small postcard with your name on it and the most incredible image of a feral battleship, its masts and cannons covered with vegetation

and your distinctively clear handwriting on the back

We spoke on the phone the week she died. She asked if I could come over, but I didn't go. I didn't have the car and I was feeling lazy, and I will always feel awful about that. The next time I saw her she was in the hospital. But she was not still. Her little arms flapped as she spoke and she had a great view of the North Hills. We talked of the hills and the few flowers that were left. She was so small in the bed.

I sat with Patricia, who was talking but then her talking changed. I couldn't understand her. What she said seemed so important and I wanted to write it down, but I had nothing. I wanted to record it. She spoke in a language that was all her own until she grew very quiet and started to groan. She was suddenly very uncomfortable. I called the nurse, but the nurse didn't come.

Patricia seemed to be growing smaller in the bed. The bed was all sheets and tubes and bone. I went home and had just poured hot soup into a bowl when the phone rang. I drove back to the hospital and passed by that stupid angel by the elevator at St. Patrick's and pushed the button and up I went, just like before, just like the time I took the elevator to see Greta but never saw her, and just as I had that morning when I first came to see Patricia. When I went into her room there were five women. They were singing

Irish Ballads and touching her. There wasn't a second when they weren't touching her. Her feet were getting cold and they told me that. I remember them touching her feet and saying how cold they were. They were crying and laughing and crying again and thought she would be so mad that she wasn't wearing red lipstick in front of so much company. But we weren't guests. These women … I've never known anything like them. They brushed her hair and they knew how to greet death.

Patricia's breathing was low, down in the wet eaves of her lungs. She seemed gone already and they said I should say goodbye, so I did. The nurse came in and told us that it would be soon. Patricia's hands were cold then and the women held them as if this would keep them warm and they began to cry and sing and they surrounded her and knew her so bone deep that I didn't feel like I should be there. They cried and as she died, I backed out of the room and walked down the hall. I just couldn't stay. The moment of her death seemed to belong to the women who had known her the longest, and who would know each other until they die—will spend their last moments together as they can. I didn't want to interrupt, or intrude. I wanted to give them the space to do what they needed to do. And I guess give myself the space to do what I needed to do.

If there was ever a settlement for pure autonomous belief, then it would have to be with these women! Who were they? Did they appear again? They sound as if they were emanations of Patricia herself, in that moment—singing to her, touching her, ushering her into ...

I do think I can name the women, but when I think of them they arrive in my mind in the form of one, morphed woman, a central figure of figures that is inhabited by all the loveliness and strength and sarcasm and toughness of Patricia. But the anonymity of these women resonates with the anonymity of the patients, flowing in the cold. They are not anonymous to someone. That is, someone knows the name and face of that person ...

I'm furious with myself for taking so long to tell you what a glorious thing of taste and beauty your broccoli soup is. I've still got some left—I'm not able to eat very much these days—but I'm looking forward to finishing it off very soon. The only problem is whether I should have it cold or hot; it's perfect both ways.

And so delicately crunchy, and deliciously spicy. It's in some ways the same, in other ways quite different, from a broccoli soup I used to make, though mine is much blander, made in the blender like yours, but with cream cheese (if I remember) and a bit of chicken stock ... very smooth and heavy. I like both of them a lot, and will send you the recipe for mine if you'll send me the recipe for yours! Then I can make yours myself, as soon as I get around to being able to take more than three or four steps at a time without collapsing.

And I was so pleased to meet your father and grandmother particularly—what an act of closure that must have been for them, however articulately—or inarticulately they may respond to it when you ask them. Your father especially looked near translucent with pleasure about the whole thing—

Congratulations, blessings always—

We said goodbye to Grams for the day. She had been sleeping, barely opening her eyes when we spoke. But she opened her eyes when we said goodbye. Poppi said, *I love you*. She mouthed back, *I love you*. He left the room to go to the elevators. Lawry and I stayed behind to talk to the doctor. When we got to the elevators, Poppi was sitting in a chair with his head in his hands, sobbing!! We were shocked as we've never seen a strong emotion from him, ever, as you know. That made us cry, and we sat with him for a few minutes.

Her arms and legs were bones. Her eyes were glassy. Her hair was a mess. She was wearing dirty clothes. Her eyes were crusty. She has no fight in her. She looks kind of peaceful, though. But she can't really talk. She can whisper a word here or there. She kept mouthing, *I want to go home!* Then she was trying to tell me something. I looked at her mouth up close to try and understand what she was trying to say, but I couldn't make it out. She would kind of mouth in a mumble, almost as if she were talking gibberish to herself. And she kept pointing to her chest. I'd ask her questions about that, but couldn't get the comprehensible answers.

I just a few nights ago attended to my granddad as he died, holding him as he breathed his last breath. A moment I've never felt before, to be so intimate with the moment of passing, and to know the moment of passing—seen no tangible way but felt, definitely and in a moment—he had had more and more trouble breathing, more and more time elapsing between breaths—when no breath would come for what seemed like far far too long, I would hold him closer and tell him that we loved him and that my folks were on their way down to see him—and the intervals between breaths would stretch on and on, and an ever more shallow breath would come, rattling with fluid building up in his chest.

A mild frenzy I notice I said, because this had been building for weeks, hell, years, hell, ten years ago when my grandmother died, he started talking about wishing he could join her under the ground.

We bought Grandad his exercise bike for his 80th birthday (1992). We'd thought it was too dangerous for him to cycle on the roads after a couple of traffic incidents and he reluctantly agreed. He also lived in a high-crime area of the city and had been mugged twice. We were worried for his health and confidence. Perhaps a stationary bike was the solution, since here was a man who was unwilling to stop moving, had been exertive all his life, a walker, runner, carpenter … He was delighted with his new acquirement and decided to travel around the world. He started logging his miles; the log included descriptions of where he went, what country, the towns and cities, barren landscapes and seas, customs, cultures and languages. When he was 89 we presented him with a silver cup—he'd actually completed 49,812 miles (equivalent to twice around the globe since he felt he'd not seen enough first time round). Subsequently, he biked pole to pole following the west coast of the Americas. He only scaled down activities when he developed Parkinson's Disease. The doctor told him to take it easy but (we discovered much later) secretly he was on the bike every day. We're not sure where he went then …

Due to failing mobility, he went to live in a residential home. He was not permitted to have a bike there. He died in 2005, at the age of 93 having traversed as many inches of the world as he was physically capable; having recreated infinite variations of nature and humankind in the equal expanses of his mind. He would bike facing a window directed southwards.

Regrettably I don't have access to his travel log. But I can tell you it was written in copperplate script and he did most definitely have encyclopaedias, many of them, often for each specific country. He was particularly entranced by Africa and South America.

I was in a room in a house, one that hasn't occurred in any of my other dreams, nor is it a house I know. I walked out of the room after being in there for a long time. I went into the bathroom and noticed that the drawers and cupboards were open, but nothing was in them. I looked into another room, and it was empty, as if someone had cleaned out the place while I was in the first room. I immediately said, *Mommy!* I was my current age.

Hiromi told me that she really hoped that you would not be offended by the part at the beginning in which she talked about your visit being a burden. She wrote it this way partly for comic effect. (She told me that when she has read that part, her Japanese audiences laugh about the houses being so small and hot, and they nod in agreement.)

Hiromi & I have talked before about the story about the mythological catfish being cut up by the god. It is clear that story is about local people in the ancient, mythological past being conquered by more advanced people coming in from the mainland Asia, perhaps Korea. The story of displacement and removal from one's indigenous place seemed to work so well with the themes of that day that she worked it into the poem.

Oh, that is such a good idea, two trees that have grown next to each other should always get married, though they might be brother and sister, or brother and brother or sister and sister, still I do not think that incest is taboo among trees, and in fact I have decided to marry a tree, this very minute I have made up my mind.

No, I never think of the pink lady when I look at the surviving portrait of my grandmother. The two paintings are completely separate in my mind. My grandmother's is all brown and dark and the Japanese lady in the kimono was all light and pink.

All things now to begin in O. I just finished my first trip through *O Bon*. I read "Crucian Carp" to Adele, who stared the sounds down with interested consternation, which evolved into a sustained growl about halfway through the poem. The growl, for her, has become a regular tool of her lexicon. Neither an angry or dismissive response, sometimes an attempt to scare, but ultimately an expression of experience that cannot find its vocabulary—thus, poetry … I read the smaller closing poem to Adele and she crawled into my lap and cuddled up and followed along on the page. When we got to the last page she she pointed at "At night, you craft your figurine/from stone" and shouted, "Airplane!" about eight times. Then, as I read on she began muttering some indecipherable incantation-babble, very much in sync with my poor rendering of your rhythms. When I closed the book she screamed again. This is highest criticism, unless maybe you can feed your book to a trout.

The past two weeks have been defined by erosion … spending time with all three of my living grandparents, seeing them all at the end of their wicks, full of regrets, bitterness, long-since-diminished visions of life's possibilities, the inability to communicate, to be honest, to be open, to express emotion, love ... all of their best-loved memories sending them back to the 1940s, the intervening years being a landscape of failures and drought. And so we found ourselves in the heart of Death Valley ... I buried *O Bon* on a hill about a body's length from where my grandfather's ashes were scattered fifteen years ago: dug a rectangular grave in the hard earth and dust and rock, lowered the book in, layered it over, looking back, couldn't see where I had buried it: it vanished instantly ... It is hard to see the horizon so clearly ... the sand dunes at the bottom of Death Valley, well below sea level, go on forever, and the moment the sun disappears behind the Panamint mountains, the sand goes cold ...

Sending you more poems than is appropriate ... To say what, in the absence of anything closer. These are all poems I wrote in Japan, this year and last. The only poems I've written in the past two years, all started in Japan, at night, in bed. Slowly transcribing them into the present incarnation. They're called, collectively, *Evening Oracle*, from a poem by Prince Niu, sixth or seventh century ...

Here's the "watermelon" poem I mentioned (attached). From what was handwritten at night in Japan, originally over a few days, though I don't now remember where. The voices came over my shoulder, then the tomb opened … Now I'm working on a poem about a woman named Etsuko. She's in her 80s, but looks much younger. She lives in the town of Kounoura, on Shodoshima Island. She paints faces on small, flat rocks. It's a hobby. The poem is "about" the rocks, or I'm thinking about the rocks. Etsuko's retired, lives alone in her house by the sea. She's very smart, has a small vegetable garden. It's circular. She lives down the road from an old stone quarry, defunct.

I want "The Japanese Apricot."

It feels like coming. I would've otherwise fed it to a statue …

We're driving out to California not this coming weekend, but the next. On that Sunday we'll get into a boat out into the Pacific to scatter my grandmother's ashes. She's a member of the Neptune Society. Then on Monday there will be the service and a reception. Then we come home. I have been staring at photos of my grandmother when she was young. As if something might assert … Her body was deeply compromised. That's many decades of eating nothing but Slim Fast. And she was tiny, a little bird. Even now a cloud has pulled over the sky … My grandfather, who had not expressed any emotion across the span of his life, broke down, started sobbing in the hall of the convalescent home where my grandmother was breathing quietly into the air above her, still living, they had just mouthed *I love you* to each other. It was a moment of redemption. One's life. Theirs. So many decades of misery and co-dependence and regret and anger and reticence. But then, one mouths *I love you* or looks out the window and sees something, and it's all vanquished, though it is all anyway. I wrote a couple of paragraphs yesterday about the stone geisha my grandmother had in her yard, her backyard. I always wondered about that woman …

We spread part of my mom's ashes in a lake near Santa Barbara, and then I spread the others in the sea off of Northern Italy. I swam through the former, not the latter. The photo of your grandmother holding your mother is amazing, though—what a beauty: her and the landscape behind her. Where in California did she live?

My grandmother was in the hospital again over the holidays while we were on the East Coast. She looked so small in the bed in the ICU there. She got better again, the doctor says she has nine lives like a cat, but each time I see her over the holidays I am not sure if I will see her again. Sometimes distance is insufferable. In any case, it is snowing here too …

My grandmother lived in the San Fernando Valley her entire life. That's where I was born: Tarzana. My sister and I. My grandmother was tiny at the end, but also at the beginning …

Today is my grandmother's funeral. Yesterday we carried the ashes of her body into the ocean. Her ashes, in the waves, became a cloud; leaning against the back railing of the boat, I turned to DD and said, *She's a cloud!* I didn't want to leave, but the boat pulled away ...

Later, we ate ice cream while standing on a bridge …

Dear Brandon, her ashes really look like a cloud, they have the melting shape of a body, though, a ghost … it somehow makes you shake, and in the picture she looks so young …

As I was walking up the stairs, I wrote, on the cover of the local newsweekly, the beginning of *The Neptune Society*. This is how it looks written, in blue pen, on the newsprint:

The moment
of redemption's
the beginning not
the end,
and
did
you
see it
subtly
waving
at the
window
a color
with no
competition
in this
life,
I think,
is over
The waving is
not a gesture
but an actual
stretch of ocean
come to ...

I neglected to tell you that the very last thing I did before I went into the hospital (I unexpectedly went into the hospital to deliver Musa, it was not yet my due date but my blood pressure had spiked—this is a long story for another (never) day) was get my hair cut ! I love getting my hair cut. I do it once or twice a year. It makes me feel newborn, or like a fresh tulip.

The person who cuts my hair is named Tomoko, and she is pregnant too! We love Tomoko because of her gentleness, and her calm. She said that in Japan you can go to temple and rub the stomach of the statue of a dog for good luck if you are pregnant. So that your delivery will be as easy as a dog's—plop, plop, plop, and there you have it, a basketful of puppies.

Why am I telling you this: I asked Tomoko what a Japanese apricot was. Then I felt immediately foolish, because 1) she looked bewildered and 2) why so literal?

Tomoko did not know about a Japanese apricot.

What about a watermelon? I said.

Watermelon?

Tomoko said: *The Japanese watermelon is very very big.*

In ~~your~~
or ~~something~~
nothing new

I saw you had
a spinach for
me? I ~~the~~ ~~something~~
~~really~~...

THE JAPANESE APRICOT

A watermelon on the back of God
Breathes through a hole in the woods

God, the gods, what shall I call them?
God, the gods
Are asleep
On a small wooden desk
In a shed, in red
Winter hats

From here I can see
A watermelon being sliced

Young monuments resemble sleep
Vice versa, the horizon
Terminated by God, the gods
Whose essence is perfect, must be
Also distant, impartial

A watermelon does not recur, not even
When definite, the watermelon never left it
Indefinite, elongates

Why do you speak of it like that?
Why do you speak like that?

We leave the shed
To walk the road

Is it we who are breathing
Through a hole in the woods?

Now only the old, neglected bell
Hanging in a cylinder of burnt wood
Needs a partner

A watermelon being sliced
Keeps the town alive
It is the being we depend on
Not what the being looks like

God, the gods
Feeding watermelon
To the small
And dysfunctional

But a watermelon on a knee is the promise
The knee belongs to someone special, might as well be that
Someone special
For whom there is nothing, no body
On which to balance

So what
Is the promise?

. . .

A mother lowers her baby
Into a flammable bisque
Baby's penis is what is called peppermint
The soul its domineering hermit

Is that what we see
In a piece of fish, curved like
An eye-patch?

The woman who brought the watermelon out
Says it is the Japanese apricot
Says it in the definitive sense

The Japanese apricot is determined
To arrive as what it arrives as

Green, with green stretch marks

. . .

I knew a girl who carried a watermelon
Eight miles over a mountain
Was she God, a god? She came down
The other side
And finished the watermelon
In a town that seemed, by all evidence, to be dead

She stood by the sink
Very still, then stopped
Moving altogether. She moved
No longer

With a buoyancy
That made me
Wonder, do stars come out first
As seeds? As if
The townspeople had left
Everything behind
And climbed like rutting
Wads of lightning

More for us, though the watermelon
Captures the dead also, realizing
The mountains begin again
At the sky   Their bodies keep moving

   is there
Earth is ending

TOHOKU

A woman is planting spinach
In the ruins of her house
Washed away white
Circles each spinach

Each circle is heat
The woman's knees touch
Her house in the form fit to give, reappearing in
The waves. There are none, it is fall

People admire the woman
Planting spinach
Where her house once stood, her age is
Mistakable

The spinach is her destiny
She does not claim its admiration
She can be the substantiation of the devil
If she wants

The spinach will grow
Will be picked and eaten
The spinach will keep growing, keep being
Picked and eaten, in each instance

The message is:
I was living, I will live, I live

The woman crouches
Without accent, an intestine among the waves
Packed with spinach, only
Partially digested

Destiny is nourished
Not the word *destiny*, but *destiny*
Is embarrassed. It too is hungry

Whatever fits in the hand
Is what is encouraged to be taken
So take it   That is what the foreigners do
They live here too, they've lived here always

SUGAWARA NO

A woman sweeps weather
From the bridge days
Later

Remembered
As one among several weathers
Eroding the bridge

A principal monument

——Don't look

Kensuke says
But in order to be here
I already have

No, you were never, the warning implies
I still have a chance
To go forward

MICHIZANE

What do you call these?
Flowers? An entire delight?

To make poems, be a scholar
Study a branch——

Did he say? I don't know
Words, exactly

Monsters and mute
And married without——

I stood on the branch
Wondering what

Made making its
Core——

It would have to be an army
A professor, a historian, a politician

For whom water flowers come

From nowhere known

And go nowhere

KEYAKI

Camphor trees swaying with children and birds
I shake the branches

The birds fly off to other trees
Children tumble to the ground

———A lady
spinning around a watchtower

spinning, and spinning
in time to evening

After taking leave of the old, spinning lady
Making me weak
Every time she slips
The scarf from her neck
                        fomenting sea monsters
We went to visit the newlyweds

95

Two trees tied the knot
And were holding the moon
Between dark green leaves, glazed savage and
A little wet
With dull excrement

Will they stay together forever?

The moon traverses
The far side of the contract

The sun displaces
The knot growing thicker

KEYAKI

When the lady breathed into
The emperor's ear
She told him everything
He previously said
Was a lie

KEYAKI

Eleven thousand times, I am a stranger
Passing artifacts, ruins, afflictions, the path
Parting from the heart, maybe

I am a girl after all the girls, I said, I mean
That is what I told her

KEYAKI

There appeared two moons
On a thin wire
Overhanging the street
      between tall trees
The moons twelve heads apart
Appeared there to be space

A man cannot dance   He feels the moons
Proposing to his partner   He kicks his partner
The hour after
The dance passes

He truly believes he is the target
His partner disappears   Who could blame her?
She was caring for a partner who could not see her

Implacable and deranged
The man pitches forward
Into a scratchy little river

HITOTSUBASHI GAKUEN

Here we are, gazing at the moon
Like all poets say
Close your eyes, and think about the light
How it will feel as you elevate your body
Knowing what will soon become of your mind
Your body, the victor, will have gone the distance
Your mind separated
Will be for the first time
Really nowhere

. . .

The sound of children singing
Thins the air
Of moon
And cloud
Umbilici

Begin   Begins over
And over the sound of children
Mocking pandemonium

TODAIJI

A child grew to be a throng
The sun shone white upon the child's faces
Only the sun could remember
One solely

Rubbing off the edge

The child woke, took its biscuits, shook itself
Over the sparkling trough
Licked green powder off a bob of ice
Took a shit in the grove

                              not sorrowful
Somewhat vengeful, the throng
Meanwhile

Stopped to admire the guardians
        naked and in flames, they had once
Been notorious, but had not aged, and so
Could not keep pace

With the throng commandeering the fury
Knowing one's self would soon go under
For a legion is polished, never more than
Is amateur

Still, there is much to admire
The trout eyebrows, the horse-like muscles
Deer moving their mouths across the guardians' feet
Pollen in ancient screws

The child's mother
Sleeps inside a guardian's foot
Scheming veins
And vegetable shadows

In her dreams, the child
Is still unable to speak, has not yet learned
The vice, yet carries a universe
On the hair of its ears

Puts itself to bed
Balances a bone on its nose
Jerks its head, the bone lands
In its mouth

Between balancing the bone
And jerking its head
The child returns like a cry
To a nightmare

NINNAJI

Eight young monks
Walk the temple grounds
Single-file
Wearing the edges of independence down
With the heart-rattling ebullience

Of babies
Eight
Young monks, a gang
Walking in perfected
Lines

Ghosts, pale-purple
Translucent
Beneath saffron robes, dollops of dirty
Rain on moles of thick
Dark moss

When you shave your head
For the first time
You will know if you are made
To be a monk
By the shape of your head

Hairs on umbrella

The unintelligible design of
Loved one's back home
Behaving like mystics on an island

It is early morning, raining
Gently
On thick, dark
Evergreens

Eight young monks, gentle
Rain, moss
Evergreens, pale
Purple, umbrella skin

Refuse to touch anything
That does not further their mission
The pagoda, for example, five stories

Neither close nor full
Enough to know
More than what they already do, from a distance

With their eyes closed

An old woman sweeps the stone steps
Where before there had not been a door
The old woman opens a door
                              strong resemblance
Is ecstasy

The temptation
To consciously perceive it, somehow
Feel it, somehow
Love it
In return

The pagoda is compact and breathless
Though I can make out a frequency
In the youth, a struggle
To possess what is real
Not what's happening

IKEDA

There is a place
I want to be
Complete, get out of the way
Its will be done, and I
Want back to it

A cock
In a cool place
Piping late afternoon
               dark walls
Of a factory

A young woman hands me
A cup of ice cream
An old woman rinsing a bucket
Sees me confused
As to where is the toilet?

Yeast is one hundred sixty years old
For all who bear themselves and die
In tranquilizing strokes
A sentence so far regarding
Little more than happenstance

A man buried in a lens of blood
Or sleeping in a lens of sweat?
Makes the hours good
To care or
Know or care to know

A cat sleeping on an old woman's foot
The old woman's foot
Bears the culture of pastry
The cat
An astringent vagina

At eleven-thirty
The noodle shop hangs its curtains
At one the noodles are gone
The gulch behind the noodle shop
Turning lubricant green

As the hills
One hundred sixty years old
      on a tongue, tasting with prescience
       is aged, though
Wouldn't it be sensible to taste it?

AKAMA

A young woman wearing large glasses
With scratched lenses
Sees everything as through a rake
No end to chores

A young woman wearing large glasses
Tennis shoes the color of tanbark
Keeps the temple grounds to herself
She does not keep herself to herself
Removes from herself one thing daily

A young woman wearing large glasses
White sweater and loose-fitting white pants
Sees everything through the margins of a cloud
Wedded to the margins of a cloud
Settling nerves on her finger

There are infinite ways to look through an insect
On the end of the young woman's nose
Wind gathering the young woman's body

KANSAI REHABILITATION

A young woman's voice
Moves through an old man's stomach
A hole will swallow
The young woman's body

Two old women fold paper into lips and ears
The young woman's voice
Folds theirs into flowers
The young woman's hands on a white synthesizer

The old man slackening beside her
No ruse, but without appetite
There's serfdom

The young woman's voice, an authenticated stroke
The old man's head
Lolls against his shoulder, turns
Upon his shoulder, and goes down

To cease an eager soul
In a body with eyes spoked
In the throat
Black sound, clearer version

TANI HOUSE

An old woman hauls herself up a steep flight of stairs
To bring sweet cakes to a boy and girl
Beneath a blue fan
On a bowed wooden wall

The stairs are in a house. The house belongs to the old woman
The stairs are the executor
The old woman is to the house as is
A letter to a dream

The last time the woman was ransacked
Her body was in large part one's misery
Someone had to stare long and hard
To imagine what could not be gotten into

. . .

The boy and girl are on the floor
Watching light cinder a broken window
Triangular leaves stain the walls
The day's porn cindering in the graveyard
Out the window, masks of low-hanging clouds
For sixteen hours, for forty hours
You will not be able to sleep

. . .

There are pictures on the wall
Of the way things used to be
Before the woman's face
Became complex
As a province
Controlled by conciliation
And self-consciousness   Smaller windows
Through which to spy people
Lightning periodically catching

A nose grows

Cauliflower
Head flowers

A head flowers in a strangers nose
Approaching an orphan

As one bereaved smells the orphan
Feeling inalienable

            decorated with bites

Flowering the odor of sun on custard

    stay human in order to melt

EGGPLANT

Someone touched a heart, became a radish
Burst, now how
Is that fatal?

I see how
Edible to touch

Commendable however, I would not be
The heart, I would be the left

Radish on the hill

I grow an eggplant plain and simple
Some are saying

Throw it through the window

KAMO

Moving invisibly through narrow streets
To catch a voice
In the hanging folds of evening

Someone is playing a flute
Someone is watching a school of fish
Eat the sound of the flute   a comet in the river
Sailing through the sun
Of a sliced face

TETSUGAKU

A mourning dove
In the moon-dry air
Drawing the sun

Swells

A friendship consecrates
A thin path
Above a narrow canal

. . .

Two women, mourning
Each other, life, the city below
Each breath, each thought
Shortly after

. . .

Two women walking side-by-side
On a thin path above a narrow canal

117

The mourning dove
Cut from the sun

Nostrils imperceptible

. . .

To be always free
Is to be always longing

To walk with yourself
Become yourself
To walk with yourself
To lose

Two eyes sputter out

. . .

I wake up early to walk with you, friend
I wake up early to become you, friend
I listen to you becoming my friend
Not *did* you hear another friend disappeared?
But *do* you hear another friend disappearing?

THREE POEMS by DOT DEVOTA

I

I start by picking things out of dirt my head
down broken tea cups shiny stubble
Shimonoseki has mild obsession with Audrey Hepburn
erase my steps temporary culture of one

we make it to Fukuoka City
a park near river a quiet canal
Brandon eating rest
of my apple hand-me down vines
bums treat me poorly granite park
bench spare cemetery feel
as if town is new and not many residents
have died yet not expecting more

Nagasaki station crowded Mayumi recognizes me immediately
that day was like going to meet up with a friend
Mayumi's one son *my life is a life for no fathers*

it feels good not to
have anything on my back
but if I am carrying

something I want it to contain everything
I own instead of only
part what owns me

after earthquake grown children
beg to return to Osaka Keiko's husband
stay and work in Tokyo do it for Japan!

II

Katsura River West Kyoto
pear wrapped in silk
story on screen a man told he should be emperor
didn't like what he heard
so he washed his ears in river needed to give cow a drink
but didn't want cow to drink now
from this dirty water
you cannot live in one hand
while opening other to show your strength
underneath Hiromi's black umbrella, Hiromi *the spirit underneath*
feels that someone I know came
be good the bamboo
is all Mandarin Oranges

a woman bent on one knee
hugging a crying toddler
toddler holds a balloon silently crying
mother motionless silently comforting
my kids are true they are with their father they are thinking
of me they are not thinking
of me I wanted to make sure—helping people
other than my family train passes
a row of two story houses an old man holds

his granddaughter on window's ledge and she
waves at people on the train passing by
natural but deliberate in morning when lotus blooms
it makes a sound:

bahmb...bahmb

III

that particular day they decided "to go look at art"
we didn't have money for exhibit
we sat in lobby at small table among case of books
sunshine increased our pain
seated by window on second floor of two story wooden school
our burns got maggots
we picked them out with chopsticks
a poplar tree begging invisible scars please tell your people
what you learned here I hope you can
imagine real hell the river
where I used to swim a bit sentimental
asking for sips

art arrives dead to artist to graveyard go thinking
I go who
is dead no place
going? art presently people want
ruptured videos with strong father lava
hardens entire mountain in cast
this can be good people don't only
want to be evident

my mind rides its bike in the same neighborhoods
how to be cast of the present? stop talking
who is tired hears dizzy night
my bell has ears inside rooms of dead houses I pass
without giving them so much food at the dinner table!
what stomachs have they to fill?
their mouths are your mouth!
flowers wrapped in newspaper cone

SHIRAKAMI

A stone resembles
A woman in white
Paused in a circle of heat
Is a man

Looking into a mirror, a mirror of stone

Some mirrors unpolished
Once reflective but aged into
Stills
Their reflections

In the old days, when the sea covered the land
White paper was placed on
The reef

Meaning, a white god worshipped
Woman and man by
The shapes of their heads
In the waves

Perfect, until they realized
They were praying to whom? To what
Absolutely resembles?

TWO MEN

Two men are roasting a dumpling
Over a low flame
In a clearing in the woods

Staring at the flame
Licking the sides of the dumpling

One man's head is significantly larger
Than the other man's head

The one man's head is swollen three times normal
The other man's head is the head of a suicide

The clearing in the woods is the perfect shape
Between the man with the head three times normal and
The man with the head of a suicide

Little malice towards each other being there
Toward themselves not being alone

Dumplings these days
Are made of railroad grass, generally

MOTOYASU

I want to sit on this bench

With this box of deep-fried pork

And eat the deep-fried pork out

Of the box

Forever

. . .

It comes quick
As I eat

Cormorants

Trooping the shallows

.

The river is

Murder, but wait
It will change, it
Can change

MOMIJIDANI

Two deer
In the river

One deer licking the other
Deer's ear

Shit
Everywhere

MIYAJIMA

Then the deer came
True, blushed
Right
To the sea

People
Came? To touch
The living? Touched
The living

To pulp   Black
Veins no longer
Ran isolated
Deer became

Horny, grew
Accustomed
To the advances of people
Naked consequences of *very* touching

Poking, peeling
A soft nose, fleshy
Then molded
A wet histrionic

People came?
The deer came
True   The tide was
That fast

MOTOYASU

Then there floated a skull
In the river

Calm
In its intelligence

That is
Seven decades of human ambivalence

. . .

A skull ignites the ears of each intelligence
You were looking for something familiar?
You were looking for some familiar thing?
Let it become a thing
To rest a head upon
The same sky dreamt, as nature is
The same standing under or understanding

. . .

The sun writes the wall

The bearer of joy

On the skin of a silent black wave

That is moving

That is still

I will share it with you

Until it is gone

EVENING ORACLE

And the pilgrimage is people
Do you see them? What do you see?

We were brought to a place
Concealed in the rush
Of people
Every one

Gone
And with them washing
A corpse ashore, as surely as

Hidden in the sky, though
Which one the ritual, which one the burial

I know we are going to say yes, we have already said yes
And I know we will not
Be able to hang
Much longer from this branch

YOKOHAMA

Today, the sea is horny with people
Upright in the waves
To the shore and arranged up
The shore among rocks overlooking the sea
Facing the shore, the hills, the rocks
Twisting out of long, flat terraces of foam

The waves reach their apex
In signatures
Lifting into the air, landing sideways
Somehow *sliding*

Open graves
Or all that
Can be taken

Sun lifting off the earth, dark earth
Waves of hair, red and black
Crawling up a supine body
Sword or gun, or however
The body's now working

Have you seen a man leap
One foot to another
Like the ground is on fire?
I have seen the ground on fire
Apparitions rising off stubble
                    planted bones in the earth
A single small wheel, inebriated and pink
The shame you feel, the shame that is relevant

The battle's beginning, one
Cheek to another
Coming out of the body, you might think
I will put myself there, make
Brides with the dead
But your thinking's a painting
Made with pestilent jellies, attracting
Black crabs to the colors

The waves reverse
Women clarify from the thousands of islands
To face the sea, to enter upright
                  remember, there are flowers
Thick, innumerable
Scrupulous gatherings
Irradiant pigment

Back home, back home, the waves
Bear flowers through white foam
Shadows of women thrown into the waves
        rise into the air, each wave closing over
The labor of past lives
Surreptitious volcanoes

The women are in the air, they are in the air
Emanating the sun, going under the sun
The deeper they inhale the sun, the closer they come
To divining the future in shadows, reflecting
The star that will become of the earth
Down the corridor of space
And the neck that is lost
You wanted to kiss, and you will

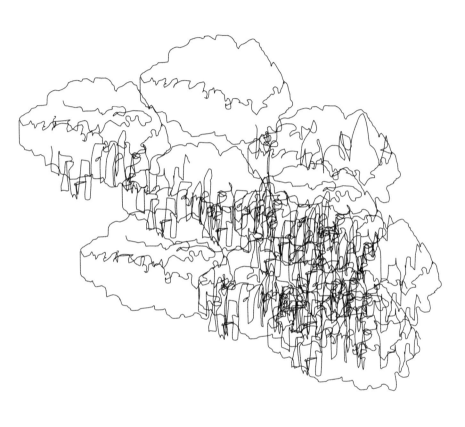

The poems in *Evening Oracle* were originally handwritten at night before sleep in the beds of friends and strangers in Japan. They were written in Dazaifu, Fukuoka, Hiroshima, Kamano, Kyoto, Nagasaki, Okukoga, Osaka, Shimonoseki, and Tokyo, in July-August 2011 and July 2012. Thank you especially to the following good and generous people for sharing their homes: Mihoko Furuya, Yoshie Honda, Yasumasa Imamura, James Jack, Mayumi Kondo, Kensuke & Machi Matsueda, Takanobu Suzuki, and Shotaro Yoshino.

Some of the poems were also written in guesthouses in Kyoto and Shimonoseki, and in Omura Kaikan Hall, Ninnaji Temple, Kyoto.

. . .

The prose passages are composed of passages from emails and letters to and from friends and family. Thank you especially to them for their continued correspondence and friendship, and permitting me to share these passages from each: Etel Adnan, Jeffrey Angles, Don Mee Choi, Phil Cordelli, Patricia Goedicke (1931-2006), Matthew Henriksen, Brenda Iijima, Youna Kwak, Quinn Latimer, Jane Lewty, Amanda Nadelberg, Mary Ruefle, Kisha Lewellyn Schlegel, Rob Schlegel, Karen McAlister Shimoda, and Karena Youtz:

But what I really wanted to tell you (Mary Ruefle). *My grandmother died this morning* (BS). *Whenever I think about my "personal" history* (Karena Youtz). *It is 9:18 in the morning in the San Fernando Valley* (BS). *Those oranges remind me* (Don Mee Choi). *Today, on the phone*

I thought I heard, for the first time (Rob Schlegel). *Your father's voice, because he touched the living wire* (BS). *Returned last night from an unexpected 6 day trip* (Rob Schlegel). *But, you all were there talking* (BS). *the trip back on Sunday* (Rob Schlegel). *We spoke on the phone the week she died* (Kisha Lewellyn Schlegel). *If there was ever a settlement for pure autonomous belief* (BS). *I do think I can name the women* (Kisha Lewellyn Schlegel). *I'm furious with myself for taking so long* (Patricia Goedicke). *And I was so pleased to meet your father and grandmother* (Patricia Goedicke). *We said goodbye to Grams for the day* (Karen McAlister Shimoda). *I just a few nights ago attended to my granddad as he died* (Phil Cordelli). *We bought Grandad his exercise bike* (Jane Lewty). *I was in a room in a house* (Karen McAlister Shimoda). *Hiromi told me that she really hoped that you would not be offended* (Jeffrey Angles). *Oh, that is such a good idea, two trees that have grown next to each other* (Mary Ruefle). *No, I never think of the pink lady* (Mary Ruefle). *All things now to begin in O* (Matthew Henriksen). *The past two weeks have been defined by erosion* (BS). *Sending you more poems than is appropriate* (BS). *Here's the "watermelon" poem I mentioned* (BS). *I want "The Japanese Apricot"* (Matthew Henriksen). *It feels like coming* (BS). *We're driving out to California not this coming weekend, but the next* (BS). *We spread part of my mom's ashes in a lake* (Quinn Latimer). *My grandmother lived in the San Fernando Valley* (BS). *Today is my grandmother's funeral* (BS). *Dear Brandon, her ashes really look like a cloud* (Etel Adnan). *As I was walking up the stairs* (BS). *I neglected to tell you that the very last thing* (Youna Kwak).

. . .

Evening Oracle is part of a family of works that includes *O Bon* (Litmus Press, 2011), also designed by HR Hegnauer.

On the first page of my songs is a strange engraving is from "Skywalk" by Gozo Yoshimasu (from *A Thousand Steps ... and more: selected poems and prose 1964-1984*, translated by Richard Arno, Brenda Barrows, and Takako Lento; Katydid Books, 1987). "O Bon" and the *Camphor trees swaying with children and birds* stanzas of "Keyaki" appeared in *O Bon*. *My greatest sorrow under heaven* is from "An elegy on the death of Prince Iwata" by Prince Niu, included in *The Manyoshu: One Thousand Poems*, trans. Nippon Gakujutsu Shinkokai (Japanese Classics Translation Committee).

The opening photograph is a screenshot of a video taken by my sister, Kelly Shimoda, of our grandmother, Jayne Seymour Nisbet McAlister (1928-2013), off the coast of southern California.

"Eels and Catfish" was written by Hiromi Ito, and translated from the Japanese by Jeffrey Angles. The three poems by Dot Devota were written in Hiroshima, August 2011. All four poems are appearing here with Hiromi's, Jeffrey's, and Dot's approvals.

The poets Dot Devota and Hiromi Ito in Nakanose, Kumamoto, July 2011

The drawing at the end of the book is of a piece of petrified wood belonging to my grandfather, Midori Shimoda (1910-1996).

Some of the poems made original appearances in/on: *BOMB, Cannibal, Diode, Mantis, Omniverse, Upstairs at Duroc, The Volta Book of Poets* (Sidebrow, 2014), and *We Are So Happy To Know Something*. Some of the original handwritten poems appeared in Sarah Lariviere's *Color Treasury*. "Hitotsubashi Gakuen" was printed as a broadside for the Fort Gondo Poetry Series in St. Louis, MO (September 2013). A version of "Tohoku" was included in the catalog for the exhibition, *Play with Nature, Played by Nature*, curated by James Jack for the Satoshi Koyama Gallery, Tokyo, April 12-May 18, 2013.

• • •

Thank you to all above, and also and again to: Baba-san, Dot Devota, Mihoko Furuya & James Jack, Annie Guthrie, Hiromi Ito & Zana Cohen, Etsuko Hamawaki, HR Hegnauer, Yutaka Iwasaki, Satsuki Kuroshima, Jayne McAlister, John Melillo & Johanna Skibsrud, Araki Nobuta, Adam Rabasca, Rob Schlegel, Karen McAlister Shimoda, Kelly Shimoda, Keiko Shirai, Joshua Marie Wilkinson, and Karena Youtz.

My greatest sorrow under heaven
My wildest grief in this world
Is that I failed to travel
With my staff or without it
Far as the clouds of heaven wander
Far as the ends of heaven and earth
To consult the evening oracle
To consult the oracle of stones …

evening oracle: form of divination from words spoken by passersby in the evening

Letter Machine Editions

Cristiana Baik & Andy Fitch, editors,
   The Letter Machine Book of Interviews

Anselm Berrigan, *To Hell With Sleep*

Edmund Berrigan, *Can It!*

Peter Gizzi, *Ode: Salute to the New York School*

Aaron Kunin, *Grace Period: Notebooks, 1998-2007*

Juliana Leslie, *More Radiant Signal*

Farid Matuk, *This Isa Nice Neighborhood*

Fred Moten, *the feel trio*

Sawako Nakayasu, *Texture Notes*

Travis Nichols, *Iowa*

Alice Notley, *Benediction*

Andrea Rexilius, *Half of What They Carried Flew Away*

Andrea Rexilius, *New Organism: Essais*

Brandon Shimoda, *Evening Oracle*

Sara Veglahn, *Another Random Heart*

John Yau, *Exhibits*